Beluga Whales

Beluga Whales

Mary Berendes

THE CHILD'S WORLD®, INC.

Library of Congress Cataloging-in-Publication Data
Berendes, Mary.
Beluga Whales / by Mary Berendes.
p. cm.
Includes index.
Summary: Describes the physical characteristics,
behavior, habitat, and life cycle of
the white whales that live in the Arctic Sea.
ISBN 1-56766-489-X (lib. bdg. : alk paper)
1. White whale—Juvenile literature. [1. White whale. 2. Whales.] I. Title.
QL737.C433B6 1998
599.5'42—dc21 97-33251
CIP
AC

Photo Credits

© A. Wambler, The National Audubon Society Collection/PR: 19
ANIMALS ANIMALS © T. Martin: 15
© Art Wolfe/Tony Stone Images: 6, 23
© Comstock, Inc.: cover
© Douglas Faulkner, The National Audubon Society Collection/PR: 24
© Gary Braasch/Tony Stone Images: 30
© Hartman-DeWitt/Comstock, Inc.: 29
© Marilyn Kazmers/Sharksong: 2, 9, 10, 16
© Mike Severns/Tony Stone Images: 20
© R. Michael Stuckey/Comstock, Inc.: 26
© Tim Davis, The National Audubon Society Collection/PR: 13

On the cover...

Front cover: This beluga whale is swimming in an aquarium in New York.
Page 2: This beluga whale is raising its head to view its surroundings.

Table of Contents

Meet the Beluga Whale!

In the icy waters of the north, penguins play and swim. Seals bark and icebergs float quietly in the sea. Suddenly, a white animal appears near the surface of the water. It blows a spray of water high into the air—WHOOSH! Then the creature quickly disappears. What could it be? It's a beluga whale!

⇐ This beluga whale is lifting its head to look all around.

What Are Beluga Whales?

Beluga (buh–LOO–guh) whales belong to the same animal group as dolphins and other whales. They are all **mammals**. Mammals are animals that feed their babies milk from their bodies. Dogs, cows, and people are mammals, too.

Beluga whales are special in many ways. They can do things that few other whales can do—such as bend their necks. They do not have a fin on their backs like some other water mammals. Without the fin, beluga whales can swim close to things such as icebergs and rocks without getting hurt.

This tame beluga whale is swimming in a Canadian aquarium. ⇒

What Do Beluga Whales Look Like?

Beluga whales are beautiful animals. Their round white bodies can bend and turn easily. They have small, dark eyes and powerful tails. They also have thick folds of fat, called **blubber**, on their bellies. Many beluga whales are about 10 or 15 feet long. Some beluga whales can weigh over 3,000 pounds.

⇐ It is easy to see the blubber on this beluga whale's belly.

A beluga whale's head is different from that of other whales. Beluga whales have a large forehead called a **melon**. Scientists think the beluga whale uses its melon to make sounds underwater. The melon changes shape when the whale is making sounds.

A beluga whale also has a strangely shaped mouth. It looks like a bird's beak! The beluga whale's mouth is called a **rostrum**. Inside the rostrum are about 40 peg-shaped teeth. The whale uses these teeth to grasp the slippery food it eats. Instead of chewing, the whale swallows its food whole.

This tame beluga is waiting for a treat from its trainer. ⇒

Where Do Beluga Whales Live?

Beluga whales live in the cold waters of the Arctic. They like to swim near icebergs while they look for things to eat. Often, beluga whales swim in very shallow water—just deep enough to cover their bodies. Here they float and rest and eat.

The beluga whale's white color helps it stay alive. The white matches the snow and ice where the beluga whale lives. Unless an enemy looks very closely, the beluga whale looks like a floating piece of ice.

These beluga whales are feeding in very shallow water. ⇒

How Do Beluga Whales Breathe?

Like other mammals, beluga whales need to breathe air. All whales and dolphins breathe through a **blowhole**. The blowhole is a hole on top of the animal's head. It is covered by a flap of muscle and skin. The flap keeps water out.

When it swims underwater, the beluga whale holds its breath. When it reaches the surface, it opens the blowhole and lets out the air. After letting the air out, the beluga whale quickly breathes in and then closes the flap.

⇐ This beluga whale has just surfaced to breathe.

How Do Beluga Whales Swim?

Beluga whales use their powerful tails to push them through the water. As the tail pumps up and down, it pushes the whale forward. On the whale's front side, two **flippers** help it to change directions. The flippers look a lot like the paddles of a small boat.

Beluga whales are very slow swimmers. They often swim only about five miles an hour. But a scared or angry beluga whale can swim up to 15 miles an hour for a short time.

This beluga whale is using its flippers to change directions. ⇒

What Do Beluga Whales Eat?

Beluga whales love to eat fish. They also like squid, shrimp, and octopus. Beluga whales are bottom feeders. That means they like to find their food near the bottom of the ocean. There they find favorite foods such as snails, crabs, and sandworms.

While they are feeding, beluga whales need to be careful. If a beluga whale isn't paying attention, a *killer whale* can sneak up and attack it. And when the beluga whale comes up for air, it must watch for hungry *polar bears* waiting above the ice. To stay safe, beluga whales need to be careful all the time.

⇐ Beluga whales often eat squids like this one.

Do Beluga Whales Stay Together?

Beluga whales often live in small groups called **pods**. The whales of a pod eat, play, and travel together. They also protect each other from enemies. Most pods are led by a large male. But some pods include only mothers and babies.

Many animals like to be left alone—but not beluga whales! They often rub up against each other or touch their flippers. Scientists think this is how beluga whales "talk" to each other. By touching and rubbing, they may be saying "Here I am!" or "Let's play!"

 This whale pod is traveling from the cold Arctic to warmer waters. ⇒

How Are Baby Beluga Whales Born?

After male and female whales mate, a baby whale starts to grow inside the female's body. The baby grows for over a year before it is ready to be born. When the time is right, female belugas travel south. Soon they find warm, safe waters. Here the females give birth to their babies.

A female beluga whale usually has only one baby at a time. It is called a **calf**. When the calf is born, it is already five feet long. It even knows how to swim! Newborn beluga whales are dark gray. As they grow, their skin gets lighter. By the time they are five years old, they finally have their white color.

⇐ This young calf is staying very close to its mother.

How Do Beluga Whales Find Their Way?

A beluga whale uses something called **echolocation** (eh–koh–loh–KAY–shun) to find its way and locate food. As it swims through the water, the beluga whale makes clicking sounds. Then it uses its melon to send the sounds in different directions. The sounds bounce off objects underwater and come back to the whale as echoes. The beluga whale listens carefully to these echoes. The echoes tell it the size and shape of objects and how far away they are.

⇐ This beluga whale is sending out sounds to find its food.

Beluga whales make many other sounds, too. In fact, they are sometimes called "sea canaries" because they sound like underwater birds! The whales use these sounds to talk to each other while they are swimming. Clucks, whistles, chirps, and squeaks are all sounds that beluga whales can make.

Beluga whales like this one can make lots of different sounds. ⇒